Poems of Love, Loss and Stardust

Charlotte Lee

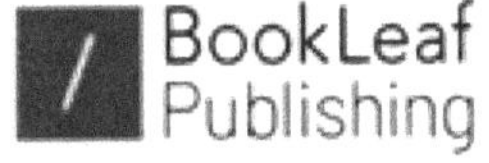

Presentation by *BookLeaf Publishing*

Web: www.bookleafpub.com

E-mail: info@bookleafpub.com

ISBN: 9789357213240

First edition 2023

Misogyny Is Alive And Well

Thank you for the Misogyny, Men.
She spent her darkest hours cowering under your
Sense of entitlement, lust for empowerment
Under your thumb she saw the beauty of your
Violence, wisteria bruises, rose petal cuts
You, the Editor in Chief of The Book of
Narcissism
A predator of daisy chain fragility, hunting
beautiful optimism
Twisted actions poison the sickly sweetness of
your words
Toxic sounds sour the careful caress of your
actions
The judge saw your sweetness,
A man with something to live for
He said she said he said she said
Your freedom choked her
Injustice, a strangulation to her sense of self
She swallowed madness to outmanoeuvre the
memories
She sliced sadness into her wisterias,
Her pain, not yours.
She was lost.

Then she was found, not by Men
She never needed Man to save her
She arose, her own Phoenix
Risen by the resentment for your chokehold
from the ashes of your assault
Your oppression caged her,
Killed her,
Spat on her soul
She towered triumphant
Queen of your chaos
So thank you for the misogyny, Men.
You made her stronger.

The Devil's Wife

Your oasis of torture
burns me to ashes, your prettiest
Phoenix in a scarlet wedding dress, hands
around my neck like a python of possession
A sick rampage of joy
Reckless abandonment in your terror
of love. We overdose
on passion, dying
in fear, in ecstasy. You cherish me
with every hit,
every kick; heaven.
Your soul as black as the bleakness of your
doings
My bruises: your favourite colour
A sanctuary of sadism, I am loyal
to my monster, I went to Hell
with a skip in my step and
a smile on my face. I knew you'd be there
waiting, your shadow dancing
I'll be your China doll when you want something
to break.
Fill my heart with venom,
crush my spirit,
my husband of Evil.

We will dance in the chaos of our conquered
Paradise.

4

Lunar Cheater

5

We were counting shooting stars
The whole galaxy: nobodies but ours
That little home we made on Mars
With the stardust roses in moonshine jars
You held me so tight in your Jupiter arms
Traced constellation love hearts over my palms
When really the daylight was screeching alarms
While your serpents' tongue silenced my qualms
For star crossed lovers are doomed to die
Our bloodied stars slipped down our sky
Murdered, brutalised, by your cheating lie
I hope in your nightmares you hear them cry
Stardust blood, oozing red
Moon's mouth open aghast, in dread
The planets weeping, mourning their dead
Are you pretending they're alive with her
instead?
Now when stargazing, I'll forever have doubt
I can't see the moon without wanting to shout
You two timed on our Galaxy, what the hell is
that about?!
Don't let the planet's retrograde burn you on
your way out.

Hummingbird Hope

Hummingbird heartbeat
Fragile foetus
You kept me alive
When I wanted so badly to
Die
Your life gave me life
That tiny hummingbird heartbeat
Of hope

Ode To A

This is an ode to the man I once adored
Despite the fact that he used my heart as a
dartboard.

You smelled of tree bark, sawdust, safety, my
home
The creases around your eyes, my favourite line
to trace
The pain in your deep dark orbs, mine to put out
You felt like heaven, my protector, my haven of
calm
We danced in your kitchen, cried on the floor
Do you remember that field? Lying on the grass,
Bathing in sunshine, tanned arms, smiles
Bubble baths wrapped in your arms
The heat, the ecstasy, the hurt, the chaos
Was that other girl worth it?

This is an ode to you, it is all I have left
You stole colour from my life, left me bereft.

We counted shooting stars, let the world around
us
stop.
Drunken karate in your sister's kitchen

We could talk for hours about Life. Death. Love.
You frustrate me like no other!
Crazy lust, crazy loathing
Perhaps because you're a Pisces, stubborn
You were my Protector, always. You turned my
safe place
Into a Dark place. Turned into my Destroyer.
Bearer of Peace, bearer of Pain
Did abandoning us make you feel better?

This is an ode to the man who ripped the heart
out of my chest
Despite all the trauma, I still wish you all the
best.

Colour Thief

I was yellow
Buttercup beacon dancing daisies hopeful happy
You were red
Crimson chaos hateful hazard searing scarlet
You sucked my colour out
I was grey
Concrete corpse sunless sallow murky moods
A colourless garden of dead despair
Lost
Then
One day
Blue
Brilliant blue
Oceans of optimism wilful waves crashing
careless clear skies smiles seagulls squawking
Green
Glorious green
Grass growing underfoot unequivocal hazy
hopeful luscious leaves lucky clover calm
Purple
Picturesque purple
Lavender lovely bees buzzing pretty petals
blowing breeze
Orange
Outstanding orange

Sunset streaked skies sandy toes tanned warmth
wanton wanderlust
You drained me, Colour Thief
So I became a damn Rainbow.

It Follows

Around the world, It follows me
That shadow that monster that Titan of
viciousness
In the kaleidoscope of Autumn leaves curled
around a Cambodian temple
In the motley of midsummer jewels on a
Croatian lake
It watches. It whispers. It wastes my sanity
In the delicacy of the moss that chokes the
spindles of the Eiffel Tower
In the ferocity of the florescence that caresses
the New York sky
It stalks. It slithers. It strangles my liberty
In the intricacy of dust floating lazily off a
Grand Canyon cliff
In the luminescence of the moonlit thunder
stroking a Thai lagoon
It haunts. It hides. It harrows my optimism
That shadow that monster that Goliath of
savagery
Inescapable, the darkness. It follows

Why Don't You Love Me?

12

Cataclysmic love, unrequited.
Fruitless adoration, dismissed.
Contemptuous disdain: heart wrenching.

Moon Don't Leave Me

This green world screams:
Will my moon lover answer my call?!
The twilight shadow of your smile
eclipses my senses.
Why did you hit me with your falling star,
blind me with the cosmic colouration of desire?
I would rip the stars out of the sky,
blow out the candle of your sunshine,
rise the dead from my oceans,
just to have your light once more.
I see your reflection in the morning dew,
watch the ghosts of our love roam my hills.
My anger tears storms through ship's sails!
I was your Earth!
I do not feel my planet burning
when the corset of your cosmos chokes me.
Whispered wishes as constant as your Northern
Star
make me miss you, my Moon.
So climb my nuclear ozone stairway to heaven.
That Galaxy cannot give you what I can.

Fly Me Away

In my dreams we are in wildest Tanzania
Sailing along the Serengeti
Sunset bathing in our adventures
Lion's roar music to our ears

In my dreams we are in Spring Paris
Hand in hand under blossom blowing
Cobblestone skipping in our romance
Eiffel Tower backdrop to our kisses

In my dreams we are in mountainous Norway
Snowdrift ski racing time of our youth
Aurora borealis emerald sky lights
Warmed by the heat in our hearts

In my dreams we are in paradise Thailand
Ocean sparkles turtle spotting
Splashes our smiles as the camera flashes
Two pairs of sandy footprints

In reality I travel alone, your shadow dancing
next to me
Gone

Phoenix Queen

Relationship gone stale
Love turned sour
Dancing in the dark with a cigarette in hand
Flicking that ash on you
You're fighting me
But I'm queen of the ashes
This love was sweet
Now it's bitter
Writhing dying screeching to end
You look cruel and callous
King of the rotten
But I'm queen of the ashes
And I will rise
You will fall
Screaming
Begging my Phoenix shadow to help you
My sour prince, you do not deserve it
I let you fall

Heartless

16

'Tis a burden on my soul
To bear the wounds of heartache
A thumping pandemonium
A dark weight in my chest
An obsolete organ
Forcing life through a ghost
No amount of pumping blood
Can stitch the tear of my crumpled soul back
together

I Miss You

The slice of a knife
The kick in the stomach
The ice through your veins
Is nothing,
Compared to the pain of loving
With an inexplicable beauty
That makes your heart soar and
Hurt with the sweetest pain
Then have it ripped away
Like tearing skin from your own body
A sword through your soul
That you keep sewing back together
You drown
People with the deepest pain
Know how to cry silently
Missing a ghost is pain defined

Hateful Thoughts

Loneliness
A strange sensation
To feel lonely when you're not alone
To be surrounded by people
yet feel empty
An ominous sadness sitting in the background of
your consciousness
Waiting patiently for when you lie awake in
blackness
You're never alone
maybe it'd be easier if you were
For you could fathom why you felt so alone
And it's not to say you don't love the people
surrounding you
Or that they're not there for you
it does not matter
You lie in their arms, safe and warm
and feel so
terribly
miserably
achingly
alone.
Your dark thoughts are your company
Your only companion at night is the grinning,
evil monster

that crouches in the corner of your mind
whispering torturing thoughts like
'why aren't you good enough?'
And
'wouldn't the world be a frightfully better place
if you weren't in it?'

Arachnid Defamation

You are a spider
Despised. Detested. Demonised.
Misunderstood
Dark little thing dancing in the shadows
Of your despair, disdain
Undeterred
You spin your web of rapture
Mighty
Dangerous little thing dextrously weaving
Your dreams, desires
Untouched by the damnation of
Your discriminators
Undamaged

Earth Ex Lover

Your meteor embrace maddened me!
Hurricane hold on my heart,
tornado tender touch
tricked me.
Do your seas still run dry?
Does your sun still cause a shiver?
Chained to your islands of devastation,
I was a tourist of your apocalypse.
Birds of paradise sing your condemnation.
Your daylight violence brings dark revelations.
Crisp autumnal daybreaks bring me to my knees
as the willow trees sway to the rhythms of your
misdeeds.
We traced smiles in the snowdrifts,
sketched love hearts in sand dunes.
Bathing in the sun streams of your sweetness
had me believing in planet-crossed lovers.
Our gravitational graveyard of secret encounters
crush my coal black cloak of self preservation.
We were flames among waterfalls:
A perfect contradiction.

Up In Smoke

My fire for you will never falter
Adoration ablaze, always
You devour my devotion
Send it up in sparks with disregard
But this pyre of passion will persist
Our white hot wildfire of wanting
Infinite inferno of intimacy
Incandescence illuminating our love
Holocaust of hazards heating our hate
Your 'sorry's' scorch my disrelish
My bonfire burns your benevolence
You are the arsonist of my abhorrence
These embers are eternal

Temporary Moments

Happiness is a butterfly
Fleeting
Flitting
Floating in my peripheral
Evading my net
Her beauty engulfs me
Swallows me
Spits me out
She lands on my shoulder
Bliss
Peace
Then off, she flies
Away

Ode To My Abuser

Damaged goods, that's what you are
Hands around your throat
your wrists
I squeeze. I like to see you
Hurt
Dirty, that's what you are
Push you down
hand over your mouth
I invade. I like to feel you
Fight
Good for nothing, that's what you are
Cigarette burns on your flesh
your pale skin
I burn. I like to hear you
Scream
Stupid girl, that's what you are
Bones sticking out of your fragile frame
hip bones, ribs
I mock. I like to make you
Sick
Unloveable, that's what you are
Blood on the sheets
tears on your cheeks
I laugh. I like to watch you
Die inside

Damaged goods, that's what you are
Silly girl, believing I'll change
love you?
I don't. I love to be your
Nightmare

Driftwood Dreaming

You dived into my dreams, dazzling drunken
sailor, saving me from a tsunami of
driftwood debris, drenching me with your
wild waves crashing wanton, we wander
over open oceans, only to orient back to
shore, surely this shipwreck shouldn't be
familiar? I feel afloat, floundering, you
caused this, creature of chaos, you crashed my
boat, bore down on my beacon, had me believe
you saved me, sea monster of storms,
mighty Midas of mayhem, mooring me to you
You are no Poseidon, no Prince, just a problem
to appear when
a damsel is adrift, darkness closing in deep
I awaken, anchor myself, come aboard
reality, yet really, when I rest my eyes, you
return
A coral kaleidoscope, a catamaran coastline of
comfort, compass confused, captured by your
cold
heart. I take the helm to harbour. I say ahoy no
more.

Saved

27

You saved me, little kick
Tiny fragile beating heart of hope
I loved you then as I love you now with the
Chokehold of knowledge that my life
Will be yours eternally, ever since I felt
That first kick